Preface

Being both a mother and a woman with a disability - for several years I have faced many challenges. I have dealt with the onset of two neurological conditions whilst being pregnant with my daughter, who is now nine years old. I then went on to have my youngest son (three years old) and recently gave birth to a healthy baby girl (4 months old.)

There were times that my illness made life frustrating, and bitter. I would have emotionally charged phases, which ultimately made me depressed and I would be lying if I said it wasn't difficult to be pregnant and disabled; the extra strain on my body, both physically and emotionally, the extra discomfort in restriction of movement and the nagging worry that my health and that of my baby may be affected.

With my first child I was already around three months pregnant when I started developing symptoms of my condition. The pregnancy and birth were normal. With my last two children, I researched into the pros and cons of having a baby in my situation and more importantly was it safe for myself and my child.

My name is Natalie Otley and this is my guide to everything you need to know about pregnancy with disability.

From the Beginning

My life was pretty ordinary prior to August 2001. I had two small boys and was relatively healthy and generally enjoying life. I was then expecting my third child. During the first trimester I began to notice I had a tendency to trip up on my left foot. I thought little of it in the beginning, but as it became more frequent and more noticeable I had no choice but to consult a podiatrist in the hope that he could locate the source of the problem.

I had seen two podiatrists in the space of two month s and had been advised by both that it was more than likely to be connected to the hormones in my pregnancy and that it would probably disappear after having my baby.

In hindsight I can see that they were taking an educated guess and had no real clue of the deeper neurological malaise that was slowly presenting itself as Multiple Sclerosis. In addition, I was also later diagnosed with focal dystonia (a movement disorder causing spasms and involuntary movements).
I progressively got worse to the point that I had to start using crutches just to stand up. Walking and standing was not possible on my left leg. The spasms became harder for me to manipulate movement in my foot.

I was referred to a consultant neurologist and further tests were performed: MRIs, Lumbar Punctures, not to mention the numerous blood tests.

Apart from the lengthy hospital waits after having just having had a baby, I was also facing the fact that I had no idea what was causing my illness. The long wait to be diagnosed was one of the most stressful parts of my illness. When it was eventually discovered that my MRIs showed lesions on the brain, it was concluded that the likelihood of me having MS or some form of demyelination was very probable. (It should be stated that there is no one conclusive test that proves a person suffers from MS, but that a series of tests are needed to indicate a reasonable probability).

As far as dystonia goes, information on this disorder is not very common place. In fact, many GPs and other medical professionals have limited information, if any, on this illness.

Dystonia is thought to be caused by a chemical imbalance in the Basal Ganglia. This is a part of the brain that controls muscle coordination and movement. The brain is dependent on the correct signals to transmit effectively. If there is a fault in the 'wiring' it often results in spasms to affected part(s) of the body. Like MS, dystonia affects the central nervous, is reliant on a number of tests to create diagnosis, and there is no cure. Though, some patients have said to have benefited from the various treatment(s) available.

For more information on dystonia and MS visit these links:

http://www.dystonia.org.uk/index.php/about-dystonia

http://www.mssociety.org.uk/what-is-ms

http://www.mumsandms.org.uk/Default.aspx

The Disabled Woman's Perspective

Women are strong. They have to be to bear children. Disabled women, it has to be said are made up of much stronger stuff; the daily challenges, both physical and emotional can often feel like a mammoth task.

Making the decision to have children can raise many issues, though some of those concerns are often purely in the discriminated mind of others.

"Would you be able to cope? How would you take care of a dependent when you are barely able to manage your own limitations?" Are the usual sometimes well-meaning questions.

Only you will have the answers and is something your doctor/health care professional provider can best advise you on.

After conducting much research I have come to learn that, though there are support groups and online communities - which undoubtedly for many provide a beacon of hope, friendship and ongoing support - there are very few publications written for the disabled mother in mind and the recent ones I have come across(post 1990-7) appear to be mainly in the US.

I wanted to write a more up-to date book easily

accessible, relevant, affordable and most importantly written with the British mother/to be in mind.

Resources need to be accessible and relevant on a local/national level. For instance, some of the paraphernalia and local sources of information in terms of equipment/health services in the cross Atlantic books obviously do not apply to the British reader.

Of course, many disabled parents find themselves dealing with the many facets of raising their children and the potential for increased anxieties. There is also the fear that this will have a marked psychological and emotional effect on their child.

There will always be those, whether part of the medical community or friends and/or family who will cast doubt upon your capability to bear your child(ren).

Of course, your ability to meet the needs of your child must always be prevalent, or to coin Great Ormond Street's motto: 'The child first and always'.

This cannot be emphasised enough: rights should always go hand in hand with responsibilities.

Many disabled people make or would prove to be wonderful parents in spite of their disabilities and restrictions. We have the advantage of being able to devote more time and attention than many able-bodied parents.

I have come to the conclusion that a great deal of the time objections are only raised from outsiders(or even those close to you) when jealousy and misinformation has risen to the surface.

The idea of anyone being jealous of a disabled person beggars belief I know, but you would be surprised.

Apart from reasons already illustrated, there are also the privileges that the disabled enjoy, ie., discounts on public services, including transport and blue badges etc and general special consideration that sadly some able-bodied just cannot handle. This is not just a case of me being bitter. Trust me I have had personal experience.

If you have bought this book then you have already made the first step towards having a little addition to your family. Perhaps you are not yet pregnant and are just considering the possibilities or have indeed already discovered you are expecting.

Either way it is vital that you receive the best care and advice from your family doctor and other medical professionals.

The First Steps

If you are seriously thinking about having a baby then now is the time to be asking yourself some important questions, such as:-

- Is it safe for you and baby. Does your disability/condition pose any threat to your self and/or unborn child by becoming pregnant?

-Would you be able to carry on taking medication whilst pregnant(and breast-feeding if you chose to do so)?

However, it is important to talk to your doctor about any medication you may be taking before trying to conceive.

Never stop taking medication until consulting your doctor.

-Would you be able to cope with the extra physical, emotional and financial challenges that come with bringing a new life into the world?

- Do you have the support of family, friends and/or local support groups?

- If you have already been pregnant before whilst disabled, would you be able to manage with another child?

- Is a subsequent pregnancy likely to flare up or exacerbate your condition as it may have done with previous pregnancies?

Obviously only you can make the decision to have a child and if you are in doubt or have serious concerns about becoming pregnant and/or raising children then seek the advice of your GP or consultant in the first place.

It is your fundamental right to raise a family. Many disabled parents have been doing so for many years and have gone on to lead healthy, constructive and fulfilled lives. It is paramount to be realistic, however, and to make sure you have equipped yourself with the facts so that you are in the best position to make an informed choice.

Of course, many disabled parents find themselves dealing with certain anxieties of bringing up their children; namely the worry that their child may have to confront complexities of having a disabled mother.

Other feelings may range from a sense of vulnerability in potential dangerous situations, i.e, their child running off and being unable to run after him/her, to a lack of understanding and sensitivity from outsiders towards the disabled. There is a fear this will have a marked psychological and emotional effect on their child. Some children, needless to say are very protective of their parents' disability, the response of others and how those people perceive that disability.

From my own personal experience I found that being upfront and open about my illness and how my disability affects me was the best way to engage them in being overt about concerns they may have and how best to address their worries.

In the Family Way

If you have already discovered you are expecting, then your first port of call is your local GP(if you haven't already done so!) and discussing your next move.

You will be given the EDD or Estimated Delivery Date of when your baby is likely to make an appearance. This is calculated from the first day of your last period. You will then be referred to your local main hospital as part of your anti-natal care regimen.

You may be able to opt for a local midwifery service attached to your local community hospital depending on where you live. I was given this option but instead went for the main maternity hospital.

Either way, you will be under the care of the consultant obstetrician whose job will be to oversee all your medical requirements and ensure you receive the best level of care.

He/she will discuss your disability and the management of any medication/treatment you are currently receiving. You may also be referred to a specialist attached to the hospital - depending on your condition and/or severity of your presentation and how often you will need to be seen.

As a disabled person you have the right to access all

public services and this includes doctors' surgeries, hospital equipment and medical/health information.

The Disability, Pregnancy and Parenthood International organisation(DPPI) is a small UK based charity, run by disabled parents. It provides a very informative, up-to-date online publication on these and many other issues relating to disability in pregnancy and parenthood. These include access to specialised height controlled cribs, beds, weighing scales, private hospital side rooms and much more.

You can download this here:

http://www.dppi.org.uk/publications/index.html

Apart from providing information on resources, experience and health reports in a free online journal, they promote invaluable sources of contact on a many number of issues relating to awareness and support for disabled people in general and in pregnancy and parenthood.

The Disabled Parents Network is also a charity-run organisation that deals with issues relating to those who are parents or hope to become parents. There is also a forum, where members can exchange ideas, share a problem, or just participate in general discussion:
http://www.disabledparentsnetwork.org.uk/

As your pregnancy progresses it is a good idea to start thinking about what you will need once the baby arrives.

Making up a list will help you organise yourself and make preparations for the practicalities, ie., buying baby clothes and equipment, as well as possibly having adaptations made to your home.

You may also want to check with your local authority to see if you are eligible for a professional helper/assistant who can help you with the day-to-day practicalities of taking care of your child and/or general domestic assistance around the home. You will need to contact Social Services and request a Health and Social Care Assessment.

An Occupational Therapist will usually be responsible in ascertaining what help you need and what level of care will be best suited to your needs.

For example, access to health care, adapted baby/child care equipment and/or help you may need around the home.

If it is felt that you would benefit from a professional home carer, your local authority will often allow you to choose and employ your own assistant and arrange payments to be made direct to your helper.

For more detailed information go to:

http://www.direct.gov.uk/en/DisabledPeople/HealthAndSupport/index.htm

Preparing for B-Day!

Time can slip away very quickly when you are pregnant and before you you know it you are only a few weeks away from the blessed event. So, again arming yourself with as much information about what to expect in delivery is essential, especially if this is your first time.

Giving birth and becoming a mum for the first time can be daunting and a little scary at the best of times, but if this is your first pregnancy as a disabled mother, you may feel yourself wanting answers to many questions that may arise as your pregnancy comes to an end.

One of the main concerns you may have is how to manage pain relief during labour. Your medical background will have to be taken into account so it is very important to discuss any worries or preferences you have with your midwife or obstetrician in advance.
These are the main forms of pain relief:-

Epidural

This is where pain-killing drugs are passed into your lower back area through a fine tube. This is a form of local anaesthesia; meaning the medicine is injected around the nerves that carry signals from that area of your body that is experiencing pain and numbs your abdomen. This is a very effective form of pain relief.

I have had three epidurals - one of which while being disabled. I found this the most beneficial and long lasting pain relief.

The only down side to it, in my opinion, was not being to feel to push the baby out(it numbs from the waist down) which can be a little frustrating.

However, you can discuss what type of epidural is best for you and whether you can allow it to wear off a little towards the end of labour, enabling you to push more effectively.

Entonox (gas and air)

This is another commonly used form of pain relief. Entonox is basically half oxygen, half nitrous oxide (laughing gas as it is sometimes called.)

This has more of a calming effect rather than actually numbing the pain completely. It takes the edge off labour pains and is safe for you and baby to use. Though it is only a mild pain killer, it is flexible (can be used in a birthing pool should you opt for this) and allows you to be in control of how little and how often you need it.

Pethidine

Pethidine is another painkiller. It works by mimicking your natural endorphins and helps you to relax. It is a synthetic form of opium and is very similar to morphine.

This drug is administered intra-muscularly and works by taking the edge off the intensity of birth pains rather than you being completely unaware of labour pain and discomfort that comes with an epidural.

Pethidine can make you dizzy, depressed or drowsy as well as nauseous. Although, the latter can be minimised by an anti-sickness injection given by your midwife.

TENS

TENS, or Transcutaneous Nerve Stimulation is a small box that you attach to your clothing. This gives out little pulses of electrical energy, via four wires leading out of the box. These wires are connected to sticky pads that are placed on your back.

It is not entirely certain how TENS work but it is believed that the electrical pulses prevents pain signals reaching your brain, or that the pulses stimulate your body's own natural feel-good chemicals called endorphins, in turn helping to block out pain.

Because it takes up to about half an hour to build up in your system, you should start using it when you are getting regular contractions.

The control settings should be started at the lowest level and gradually increased as your contractions and/or back pain becomes more intense.

TENS can be hired for up to seven weeks from http://www.pregnancy.co.uk

The cost is £17.95 and is the cheapest I have come across to date. The price includes first class delivery and free return included - plus free practice electrodes that would normally cost around £5 from other outlets.

Make sure you check with your obstetrician/specialist before using TENS as it may interfere or be unsuitable for your medical condition(s). i.e., particularly if you suffer from epilepsy/ other neurological or cardiological illness.

TENS is rarely given at hospitals as women are only usually admitted when they are in established labour. TENS is most effective when it is taken at the onset of pains.

Established labour essentially means the active

phase of the first stage of labour. This is when the contractions become stronger and closer together.

The advantages of TENS is that it is portable, under your control and easy to use. The down sides are that it may only help if used in early stages of labour, it may need to be removed in the case your baby's heart needs to be monitored electronically and can only be used in a birthing pool BEFORE you get in the water and not during.

It should be noted that if you feel it is not helping you, simply take it off and ask for another method of pain relief. This is still open to you.

You can find out more about the issues already mention and other topics relating to pregnancy and birth, from the NHS' own website dedicated to these important health concerns and a great deal more at http://www.nhs.uk/Planners/pregnancycareplanner/Pages/during.aspx

Here you will be able to access a Pregnancy Planner tool that gives invaluable information on many subjects relating to your pregnancy and how best to organise yourself with weekly-to-do lists, how to write a birth plan, choosing where to have your baby, choosing your antenatal care and also has a pregnancy blog where mothers-to-be talk about their pregnancy experiences. I was very impressed with the information and layout of the site. It's well worth checking out.

The other things you will also need for your baby are:-

8 Body vests

2 Baby socks

Pram suit

1 pack of nappies

Baby wipes

Cotton balls

Baby bath (you may need to contact your local authority should you need specially adjusted baby equipment)

Baby thermometer

Breast pump for expressing baby milk

Steriliser for baby's bottles and accessories

Moses basket

Fitted sheets

Baby blankets

Baby monitor

Pram

It is vital that you have everything prepared for when you need to go into hospital. Having a bag packed with all the essentials for you and baby takes that extra weight off your mind and will make you feel more at ease.

I found buying a pre-packed hospital bag really useful(off Ebay)It had almost everything I needed (I just added some things that were not included.)

I recently found two very good sites where you can buy pre-packed bags.

Baby Mama Bags have a good range of affordable and stylish bags, loaded with all the things you and your baby will need during your stay in hospital. They also sell baby changing bags too.

http://www.babymamabags.co.uk/default.aspx

Isyourbagpacked has a very wide range of products for mums and babies. Certainly takes the strain off going here, there and everywhere. Most of what you will need is all in one place.

http://www.isyourbagpacked.co.uk/index.asp

Exercising in Pregnancy

The right balance of nutrition and general exercises in pregnancy is very important in determining the healthy outcome of your pregnancy. It also helps to prevent any complications prior to giving birth.

Exercising for disabled women, in particular can be of added benefit. For example, stretching after exercising or even simply after having a warm shower, can help prevent muscle spasms, swimming, which can promote good circulation and muscle flexibility etc.

I have come to realise after conducting research for 'The Disabled Mother's Guide..' that there is very little information about exercising in pregnancy specifically geared towards disabled women. This clearly needs to be addressed as many women find this lack of information frustrating and often feel isolated as a result.

I have come across some very basic specific exercises aimed at disabled mothers. These include Pelvic Tilts, Sit-ups, Muscle Strengthening Leg lifts and Deep Breathing.

These can prove very beneficial particularly for those ladies who suffer from joint and muscular conditions.

As with all medical treatment the advice and support of your local health care professional is imperative and physical therapy is no exception. The exercises that I discovered were very generalised. Each person is different and you will need to get the advice of a trained physiotherapist to work out what is the best exercise regime for you .

With my recent pregnancy I was given a contact number of the physio department where I could make a self-referral.

I found this service very useful and extremely beneficial. I was seen within a week and was given practical advice on how to manage my mobility and pregnancy at the same time.

Depending on where you live in the UK and which hospital/birth centre you are with, self-referrals are proving very popular and quite widely used.

If your hospital does not offer this service then your local GP should be able to assist.

You can find more information here: http://www.nhs.uk/Conditions/Physiotherapy/Pages/Accessing-physiotherapy.aspx

As your pregnancy draws to a close you should have a

clearer picture and a structured plan in place as to how you will have your baby, i.e, hospital, birth centre or home birth, which form of pain relief you will opt for, who will be with you at the birth (your partner, or other relative/friend) and any practical/medical needs that the midwifery team and doctors should be made aware of during the course of your stay in hospital etc.

Always remember:never be afraid to ask for help from your midwife or doctor.

Life After Pregnancy

Ok, so you have done all the hard work, nurtured, protected and gave your child life.

You are now a proud mother - perhaps for the first time.

You will be spending a great deal of your time getting to know your new baby.

This period is truly magical and very rewarding. The bond that you develop with your child is a special one, perhaps more so being disabled;you may have more time to devote to your baby due to mobility restriction(s), this period of time will become more focused as he/she grows older and their needs increase accordingly.

It is hard work in the beginning. There will be days when you are irritable, exhausted and generally fed up with not getting enough sleep, but the love and joy that you feel for your baby far out-weighs the discomfort you may experience.

Not all new mothers share 'maternal euphoria' -as I like to call it- after giving birth. Many women experience PND, or Post Natal Depression. This affects 10-15 out of every 100 women.

It is important to take time for yourself too after

childbirth.

Don't underestimate the importance of recognising the signs of PND, shrugging it off as "baby blues".

If you feel any, or all of the following symptoms, seek advice from your GP or health visitor:

Low mood
Loss of appetite
Loss of interest in yourself or the baby
Crying all the time
Panic Attacks and anxiety
Hiding how you feel and "putting on a brave face".

These are just a few classic symptoms to be aware of.

The Royal College of Psychiatrists has a very useful fact sheet on PND and how to seek help.

Don't let the title put you off as it may sound too 'clinical' to you.

The RCPsych provide very beneficial advice and information on the different treatments available - plus a self-help section.

There are many useful contacts and links on this fact sheet. Well worth checking out!

http://www.rcpsych.ac.uk/mentalhealthinfoforall/problems/postnatalmentalhealth/postnataldepression.aspx

Sometimes, with some mothers, it is simply a case of the constant crying and finding a way to adjust to motherhood and their new baby.

Cry-sis provides self-help and support for families with excessively crying, sleeplessness and demanding babies.

Tel: 08451 228669.

ttp://www.cry-sis.org.uk/

It has to also be stressed, at this point, that mental illnesses are also recognised as a disability, though many are ignorant of this fact.

If you have suffered from depression/mental illness before or just after giving birth with any previous pregnancies, you are at a higher risk of developing PND

Again, there is help available for women who fall into this category.

The following links provide excellent information and support.

Remember that you can always enquire with your GP or health visitor about any of the services that you may feel would be of benefit to you.

http://www.nhs.uk/Livewell/mentalhealth/Pages/gethelp.aspx
http://www.nhs.uk/Livewell/mentalhealth/Pages/Helplines.aspx
http://www.direct.gov.uk/en/DisabledPeople/HealthAndSupport/MentalHealth/DG_10023343
http://www.direct.gov.uk/en/Dl1/Directories/UsefulContactsByCategory/DisabledPeopleContacts/SpecificNeedsContacts/DG_10014900
http://www.nhs.uk/carersdirect/guide/mental-health/pages/emergency-mental-healthcare.aspx
http://www.nhs.uk/Tools/Pages/Longterm.aspx

These are some other sites that you may find especially helpful for PND and mother and child issues in general:-

http://www.mothersformothers.co.uk/

http://www.askamum.co.uk/

http://www.nct.org.uk/

Other help

The organisation Home Start provide confidential, non-judgemental help and resources for families with at least one child under five and in need of assistance for whatever reason. You may need practical help for instance, getting a break during the day, or help with parenting problems you may have experienced.

Perhaps you need some advice on how to access resources that can help with a ny problems you have encountered as a family, or maybe you could just do with someone to speak to about any issues you may have to do with parenting, covering a wide area.

Home start can put you in touch with volunteers (all have an enhanced level criminal records check) who can help in a many number of ways.

Go on to the web site for more details.

http://www.home-
start.org.uk/needsupport/need_support

Free info line: 0800 068 6368

There is some truth in the cliche- it gets easier as they get older!

As your child grows and develops into a toddler and then onto a more independent child, you will find that you are more able to interact and communicate on a higher level, sharing an awareness of "Mum's disability" and learn to love and help you as their mother as you, indeed help them to grow into adulthood.

The Next Stage

Before you know it, your baby will reach the stages of crawling and walking. In time you will also discover ways to best care for your child that works for you.

Some of the difficulties that many mothers encounter are the practicalities of raising their children in a safe and hassle-free environment.

This can be anything from bath and changing time to feeding, playing and later on introducing restraint when their toddlers are having a tantrum outside, for example, or perhaps being able to control their child from misbehaving in public and running into the road.

There are practical measures that you can implement in order to be able to take care of your child with ease; taking the strain out of any restrictions that you may come across since becoming a disabled mother.

There is a wealth of information on how to adapt your home, get help with adjustable baby equipment that are tailored to suit your needs and general advice on how to access the best resources and support - through NHS/social services, or through the private sector.

Go to the following links for more:

http://www.direct.gov.uk/en/DisabledPeople/Disabledparents/DG_10037907
http://www.direct.gov.uk/en/Dl1/Directories/UsefulContactsByCategory/DisabledPeopleContacts/OrganisationsAndCharities/DG_10014866
http://www.dlf.org.uk/factsheets/Disability_pregnancy_and_parenthood.pdf

Ricability provides a Watch Dog type of report on the best products for disabled parents, such as highchairs, safety gates and baby carriers. http://www.ricability.org.uk/consumer_reports/parenting/

Whilst researching for this book I came across a height adjustable standing frame called the Funpod by Little Helper. It enables your child to eat at a high place, which is great for feeding and playing as it brings the child to your level. It works by having completely enclosed sides, allowing your toddler to stand in it and reach counter-top, so he can help or play alongside you in the kitchen.

http://www.littlehelper.co.uk/shop.php

Now, these Fun Pods are very nifty but also quite pricey. You can get them on Ebay(last time I checked) for a substantially price.

There is also the worry when going out with your child that he may run off. There is always a fear that you won't be in the position to prevent him from running off into a busy road. The solution, quite simple is reins. Many people feel strongly about the use of reins because it is often likened to dog leashes. Your child's safety and your own peace of mind are paramount. I don't believe any parent would want to put themselves and child in a position where their safety is being compromised,especially in a public place.

Granted, the wrist reins are a little disconcerting and not something I would personally endorse. I feel they are not very safe and may even cause injury if there is a fall, for example. There are harness reins which are attached to a little backpack your child wears. There are many designs for both boys and girls and affordable.

Kiddicare have quite an extensive range:

http://www.kiddicare.com/webapp/wcs/stores/servlet/categorydisplay10A_265_10751_14769_-1__14054_14054_10001_14054?rw.cm=Google,ppc,baby+reins+with+rucksack&cm_mmc=icrossing-_-Google-_-nursery+online-_-baby+reins+with+rucksack&OVMTC=Exact&site=&creative=9338135053&OVKEY=baby%20reins%20with%20rucksack&url_id=10608735

If you have a partner, let them share the responsibility in giving you that much needed help indoors and out. Do things together as a family. Your child needs to experience love and affection from you as their mother, but should be mindful that with love comes discipline and the importance of good behaviour. Your child also needs to realise that you have support from your other half and other family members.

Here are some other useful tips I came across recently, showing that sometimes the simplest ideas can prove helpful. Grabbers are useful in reaching that stray toy, or fallen soother you just can't reach!Some mothers find it particularly trying when their children start taking advantage of they new found independence, testing how far they can push mum.

All children are naughty from time to time and finding a method that works for you is key to resolving any practical obstacles to disciplining your child.

Try introducing a carrot and stick approach to a wayward toddler if you are finding it particularly difficult in physically lifting him off the floor when he's kicking off.

Why not use a sticker chart and reward your child

with a treat after he has earned, say 10 stickers for good behaviour, only allowing these treats if he has acted according to your wishes.

Or, try taking a favourite toy out with you when you are taking him somewhere. If he misbehaves, then you distract him with the toy; alternating with different toys whenever you go out.

Basic adaptations to your home, enabling you to care for yourself and child also makes an enormous difference to your day-to day life. Hand rails, adaptations to the home etc, will be provided by your local authority once you are assessed and a need for care and support is ascertained.

An Occupational Therapist can offer much needed assistance, particularly around the home.

Follow this link to find out how this service can help you:

http://www.direct.gov.uk/en/DisabledPeople/HealthAndSupport/ArrangingHealthAndSocialCare/DG_4000436

You will find your own ways to raise your child; with or without outside help. Only you know what works for you and your family. You are the authority in what your limitations are and what is feasible to achieve.

I realised after losing my mobility and later having children whilst being disabled, that there are many issues faced by disabled parents on a day-to day basis ; that we have challenges we must overcome in order to provide the best for our children.

To be quite frank, when I was mobile, I never imagined how hard it can be at times for others who have a disability. Never giving it a second thought. Nor did I ever contemplate being a disabled pregnant mother three times.

As my pregnancies developed, I did feel the strain sometimes of my hormones playing havoc with the emotional task of caring for myself and unborn child. Feelings of anxiety and protectiveness, mixed with joyful anticipation would be how I would sum up my experiences of learning that I was to be a mother again, but with the extra challenge and responsibility of being disabled with it.

It can be done. Disabled women can have children. Many have done so and have gone on to make wonderful, loving parents.

You will find, as did I, that your child(ren) will be very protective of you and will appreciate that you may have days when you are not on top form. That they learn to understand you and appreciate even the small things you do. You will also feel closer to your children and they will to you. They will look to you for guidance and strength. What greater strength is there then proving you can embrace the challenge of parenthood and being the best you can.

I feel blessed that I have been given the opportunity to prove that it is not only possible but a privilege. Mine has been a journey of discovery, uncertainty, fear and joy. There have been many tears along the way, but also much laughter and positivity.

I hope that after reading this book you will find some use from the advice contained within it.

<u>On a final note</u>:

Many disabled women feel there is a lack of information on disability, during and after pregnancy, what to expect and what is available to them. While things have changed within the last several years, there is always room for improvement. We have to be a part of that change. By educating others, especially in the medical field, on what it is like to experience the sometimes physical strain of disability, but also the determination to lead a normal life as possible. This is the first step. There are many charities and other organisations who are very active in promoting disabled rights. The places that I have recommended are a good place to start.

Attitudes still need to be changed, but we can only do this by empowering ourselves and showing others what we are able to achieve and how we have made accomplishments that some would never believe possible.

One of those is successfully raising our own family!

Useful links:

http://www.direct.gov.uk/en/DisabledPeople/Disabledparents/DG_10037841
http://www.dppi.org.uk/links/index.php#35
http://www.direct.gov.uk/en/DisabledPeople/RightsAndObligations/index.htm
http://www.mumsandms.org.uk/Default.aspx
http://www.turn2us.org.uk/about_us/our_purpose.aspx
http://www.bda.org.uk/
http://www.qefd.org/
http://www.disabilities-trust.org.uk/
http://www.scope.org.uk/
http://www.lifeways.co.uk/
http://www.edfwomen.org.uk/
http://www.dlf.org.uk/
http://www.remploy.co.uk/
http://www.disabilityalliance.org/
http://www.disabilitynow.org.uk
http://www.disabilitywales.org/
http://www.opsis.org.uk/
http://www.spinal.co.uk/

http://www.mssociety.org.uk/
http://www.arthritiscare.org.uk/Home
http://www.epilepsy.org.uk/
http://www.equalityhumanrights.com/
http://www.direct.gov.uk/en/DisabledPeople/index
.htm

www.ingramcontent.com/pod-product-compliance
Ingram Content Group UK Ltd.
Pitfield, Milton Keynes, MK11 3LW, UK
UKHW020215250726
13967UKWH00001B/2

9 781471 047930